Crescent Roll Recipes

Copyright ©

All rights reserved. No part of this book may be reproduced, stored in a retrieval system, or transmitted in any form or by any means, electronic, mechanical, photocopying, recording, scanning, or otherwise, without the prior written permission of the publisher.

Disclaimer

All the material contained in this book is provided for educational and informational purposes only. No responsibility can be taken for any results or outcomes resulting from the use of this material.

While every attempt has been made to provide information that is both accurate and effective, the author does not assume any responsibility for the accuracy or use/misuse of this information.

Crescent Wrapped Brie

Ingredients:

1 (8-oz.) can Pillsbury® Refrigerated Crescent Dinner Rolls or Pillsbury® Crescent Recipe Creations™ Flaky dough sheet1 (8-oz.) round natural Brie cheese
1 egg, beaten

Directions:

Heat oven to 350 degrees F.

Crescent Rolls: Unroll dough; separate crosswise into 2 sections. Pat dough and firmly press perforations to seal, forming 2 squares.

Recipe Creations: Unroll dough and cut crosswise into 2 rectangles. Pat dough to form 2 squares. Place 1 square on ungreased cookie sheet. Place cheese on center of dough.

With small cookie or canape cutter, cut 1 shape from each corner of remaining square; set cutouts aside.

Place remaining square on top of cheese round. Press dough evenly around cheese; fold bottom edges over top edges. Gently stretch dough evenly around cheese; press to seal completely. Brush with beaten egg. Top with cutouts; brush with additional beaten egg.

Bake at 350 degrees F. for 20 to 24 minutes or until golden brown. Cool 15 minutes. Serve warm.

If using Pillsbury® Big & Flaky large refrigerated crescent dinner rolls, unroll dough and press into 1 rectangle, sealing perforations. Cut in half, forming 2 squares. Continue as directed--except add 8 to 10 minutes to bake time.

Green Bean Casserole Crescent Cups

Ingredients:

2 cans (8 oz each) Pillsbury™ refrigerated crescent dinner rolls

1 (10 oz) condensed cream of mushroom soup

½ cut cup milk

1 teaspoon Worcestershire Sauce

2 cans (15 oz each) green beans, drained

1 cup shredded Cheddar cheese

1 ½ cups French-fried onions

Directions:

Heat oven to 375°F. Lightly spray 16 regular-size muffin cups with cooking 11spray.

Unroll each can of dough. To make 2 large rectangles, pinch seams and perforations to seal. Cut each rectangle of dough into 8 equal squares. Line each muffin cup by pressing 1 dough square in bottom and up sides of cup.

Unroll each can of dough. To make 2 large rectangles, pinch seams and perforations to seal. Cut each rectangle of dough into 8 equal squares. Line each muffin cup by pressing 1 dough square in bottom and up sides of cup.

In large bowl, stir together soup, milk, Worcestershire sauce and dash ground black pepper with whisk until smooth. Add drained green beans, 1/2 cup of the cheese and 2/3 cup of the onions; gently stir until combined. Divide mixture evenly among dough-lined cups.

Bake 12 to 15 minutes. Remove from oven. Divide remaining cheese and onions evenly onto tops of cups. Return to oven; bake 5 minutes longer or until onions and cups are golden brown. Cool in pan 5 minutes. Serve warm

Sausage Crescent Cheese Balls

Ingredients:

1 lb bulk spicy sausage

2 cups shredded sharp Cheddar cheese (8 oz)

½ teaspoon dried rosemary leaves, crushed

1 can (8 oz) Pillsbury™ refrigerated crescent dinner rolls

2 tablespoons all-purpose flour

Directions:

Heat oven to 375°F. Line 15x10x1-inch pan with foil; spray with cooking spray.

In large bowl, mix sausage, cheese and rosemary; mix well using hands or spoon.

Unroll crescent dough on work surface; coat each side of dough with 1 tablespoon flour. Using pizza cutter or knife, cut dough into about 1/4-inch pieces. Mix crescent dough pieces into bowl of sausage mixture in small amounts until well blended.

Shape mixture into 42 (1 1/4-inch) balls. Place in pan. Bake 15 to 17 minutes or until golden brown.

3-Ingredient Sausage-Cream Cheese Crescent Bundles

Ingredients:

½ lb bulk hot pork sausage

½ cup spicy jalapeño cream cheese spread (from 8-oz container)

1 can (8 oz) Pillsbury™ refrigerated crescent dough sheet or 1 can (8 oz) Pillsbury™ refrigerated

Directions:

Heat oven to 375°F. In 10-inch nonstick skillet, cook sausage over medium-high heat 4 to 5 minutes, stirring frequently, until no longer pink; drain

Unroll dough on work surface. Press into 12x9-inch rectangle. If using crescent roll dough, firmly press perforations to seal. With pizza cutter or sharp knife, cut into 6 rows by 4 rows to make 24 squares.

Place about 1 rounded teaspoon sausage on center of each dough square. Top with about 1 teaspoon cream cheese. Bring 4 corners together to overlap slightly in center at top of each bundle. Twist and pinch to seal, leaving small gaps between seams. Place on ungreased cookie sheets..

Bake 10 to 14 minutes or until golden brown. Serve warm.

Buffalo Chicken Crescent Ring

Ingredients

4 oz cream cheese (half of 8-oz package), softened

¼ cup hot sauce or red pepper sauce

2 ½ cups chopped cooked chicken (1/2-inch pieces)

1 cup shredded Monterey Jack cheese (4 oz)

2 cans (8 oz each) Pillsbury™ refrigerated crescent dinner rolls

1/3 cup crumbled blue cheese

Directions:

Heat oven to 375°F. In small bowl, mix cream cheese and hot sauce until smooth. Mix in chicken and shredded cheese just until combined.

Unroll both cans of dough; separate into 16 triangles. On ungreased large cookie sheet, arrange triangles in ring so short sides of triangles form a 5-inch circle in center. Dough will overlap. Dough ring should look like a sun.

Spoon cream cheese mixture on the half of each triangle closest to center of ring. Top with blue cheese crumbles.

Bring each dough triangle up over filling, tucking dough under bottom layer of dough to secure it. Repeat around ring until entire filling is enclosed (some filling might show a little).

Bake 20 to 25 minutes or until dough is golden brown and thoroughly baked. Cool 5 to 10 minutes before cutting into serving slices.

Cinnamon Roll Bites

Ingredients:

12 oz. can refrigerated biscuits

3 TB butter, melted

⅓ cup sugar

1 TB cinnamon

Glaze:

1 cup powdered sugar, sifted

2 TB butter, melted

1 tsp. vanilla

2 TB milk

Directions:

Preheat oven to 350.

Grease 8x8 pan.

Place cinnamon and sugar in a small bowl and mix well. Set aside.

Cut biscuits in 4 and dip in cinnamon/sugar mixture until coated.

Place in pan close together and spread melted butter over cut biscuits.

Bake for 20-22 minutes.

Cinnamon Crescent Twists

Ingredients:

2 TB sugar

1 tsp. ground cinnamon

1 can (8 oz) crescent rolls

3 TB melted butter

Directions:

Preheat oven to 375.

Unroll your crescent dough and lay down as 4 rectangles on a greased cookie sheet making sure you press the triangles together to form the rectangles.

Mix together your sugar and cinnamon in a small bowl and set aside.

Spread melted butter onto 2 of the rectangles and sprinkle a little less than half the cinnamon/sugar mixture onto those rectangles.

Take the two non-buttered rectangles and put those on top of your buttered and cinnamon/sugar rectangles. Press edges together.

Cut both triangles into 6 strips and top with any reserve melted butter. Twist each strip a few times and spread onto cookie sheet.

Sprinkle with remaining cinnamon and sugar.

Bake for 8-10 minutes.

Pecan Bars

Ingredients:

1 can (8 oz) refrigerated crescent rolls

3/4 cup chopped pecans

1/2 cup sugar

1/2 cup corn syrup

2 Tbsp butter or margarine, melted

1 tsp vanilla

1 egg, beaten

Directions:

Heat oven to 350°F.

Unroll dough and press in bottom and 1/2 inch up sides of a 9x13-inch pan. Firmly press perforations to seal. Bake 8 minutes.

Meanwhile, in medium bowl, mix remaining ingredients. Pour filling over partially baked crust.

Bake 18 to 22 minutes longer or until golden brown.

Cool completely, about 1 hour, and cut into bars.

S'mores Monkey Bread

Ingredients:

½ cup sugar

½ cup crushed graham crackers or graham cracker crumbs

2 cans (16.3 oz each) Pillsbury™ Grands!™ Flaky Layers refrigerated Original biscuits

1 cup milk chocolate chips (6 oz)

½ cup miniature marshmallows

1 ¼ cups marshmallow creme

¾ cup butter

1 teaspoon vanilla

Directions:

Heat oven to 350°F. Spray 6-cup (9-inch) fluted tube cake pan or angel food (tube) cake pan with cooking spray.

In large food-storage plastic bag, mix sugar and cracker crumbs.

Separate each can of dough into 8 biscuits; cut each into quarters. Place 6 to 8 biscuit pieces in sugar-crumb mixture; shake well. Continue to add more biscuit pieces to sugar-crumb until all are completely coated.

Layer biscuit pieces, chocolate chips and marshmallows in pan.

In 1-quart saucepan, melt marshmallow creme, butter and vanilla over medium heat. When mixture begins to boil, cook and stir 1 minute. Pour over biscuits, chips and marshmallows in pan.

Bake 35 minutes or until golden brown. Cool in pan 10 minutes. Place plate upside down over pan; turn plate and pan over. Remove pan. Serve warm.

Gouda Bites Recipe

Ingredients:

1 tube (8 ounces) refrigerated reduced-fat crescent rolls

1/2 teaspoon garlic powder

5 ounces Gouda cheese, cut into 24 pieces

Directions:

Unroll crescent dough into one long rectangle; seal seams and perforations. Sprinkle with garlic powder. Cut into 24 pieces; lightly press onto the bottom and up the sides of ungreased miniature muffin cups.

Bake at 375° for 3 minutes. Place a piece of cheese in each cup. Bake 8-10 minutes longer or until golden brown and cheese is melted. Serve warm. Yield: 2 doz

Faux Cronuts

Ingredients:

1 tube of Pillsbury Big and Buttery Grands Crescent Rolls

Canola Oil for Frying

1/2 cup Sugar mixed with 1 tsp cinnamon

Directions:

Heat your oil over med - med/high {make sure you use a large pot to prevent splashing}

While the oil is heating, roll each crescent triangle {beginning with he short side} into a loose rope, and then form your circle {making sure to tuck the ends together to seal them}

Fry them one at a time {about 1 minute on each side}

Drain on a paper towel or brown paper bag

Dip both sides in the cinnamon sugar

Taco Pops

Ingredients:

1 can (8 oz) Pillsbury™ refrigerated crescent rolls

1 cup prepared taco filling15

lollipop sticks

Salsa, queso, sour cream, guacamole for serving (optional)

Directions:

PREHEAT OVEN TO 375 DEGREES

Roll out the crescent roll dough in a sheet, and just pinch the precut edges back together

Cut into three long strips, lengthwise, and then in five, to make 15 squares. Spoon a little bit of taco filling on each square. Pinch the edges up, to make a little purse and enclose the filling. Roll quickly between your hands to smooth.

Bake at 375°F for 11 to 13 minutes, until golden brown.

Taco Cupcakes

Ingredients:

1 pound ground beef

(1 oz) package taco seasoning mix

2/3 cup water 1 can (16 oz) refried beans

36 tortilla chips

2 cups shredded cheddar cheese

Optional toppings: sour cream, diced tomatoes, cilantro, onion

Directions:

Preheat the oven to 375°F. Spray 18 muffin cups with cooking spray.

Brown beef in a skillet and drain the fat. Add the taco seasoning mix and water, and simmer for 4-5 minutes. Set aside.

Place one wonton wrapper in the bottom of each muffin cup. Layer about 1 tablespoon of refried beans on top of each wonton. Crush one tortilla chip on top of the beans. Top with 1 tablespoon of taco meat and 1 tablespoon of shredded cheese. Repeat the layers again with a wonton wrapper, refried beans, tortilla chips, taco meat and cheese.

Cream Cheese-Bacon Crescents

Ingredients:

1 tub (8 oz.) Chive & Onion Cream Cheese
3 slices cooked Bacon, crumbled
2 cans (8 oz. each) refrigerated reduced-fat crescent dinner rolls

Directions:

Heat oven to 375°F.

Mix reduced-fat cream cheese and bacon until blended.

Unroll crescent dough; separate each can of dough into 8 triangles. Cut each triangle lengthwise in half. Spread with cream cheese mixture, adding about 1 tsp. cream cheese mixture to each triangle.

Roll up, starting at short side of each triangle.

Place, point sides down, on baking sheet.

Bake 12 to 15 min. or until golden brown. Serve warm.

Quick Cold Vegetable Pizza Recipe

Ingredients:

2 tubes (8 ounces each) refrigerated crescent rolls
1 cup mayonnaise
1 package (8 ounces) cream cheese, softened
1 tablespoon dill weed
2-1/2 cups mixed chopped fresh vegetables (cucumber, radishes, broccoli, onion, green pepper, carrots, celery, mushrooms)
1/2 cup sliced ripe olives
3/4 cup shredded cheddar cheese
3/4 cup shredded mozzarella cheese

Directions:

Unroll the crescent rolls and place in an ungreased 15-in. x 10-in. x 1-in. baking pan. Flatten dough to fit the pan, sealing seams and perforations.

Bake at 375° for 10 minutes or until golden brown.

Cool in a small mixing bowl, beat the mayonnaise, cream cheese and dill until smooth; spread over crust.

Top with the vegetables of your choice. Sprinkle with olives and cheeses; press lightly.

Cover and chill for at least 1 hour. Cut into squares.

Yield: 12-15 servings.

Festive Fiesta Bites

Ingredients:

1 can (8 oz.) refrigerated crescent dinner rolls
1/4 tsp. ground cumin
1/4 tsp. chili powder
1/2 cup (1/2 of 8-oz. tub) PHILADELPHIA Cream Cheese Spread
3/4 cup guacamole
1 small tomato, seeded, finely chopped
1/4 cup pitted black olives, finely chopped
1/4 cup OSCAR MAYER Real Bacon Bits
1/4 cup finely chopped fresh cilantro

Directions:

Heat oven to 350°F.
Separate crescent dough into 2 rectangles; firmly press perforations together to seal. Place, 2 inches apart, on baking sheet sprayed with cooking spray; sprinkle with seasonings.
Bake 15 min. or until golden brown; cool. Mix cream cheese spread and guacamole until blended; spread onto crusts.
Top with remaining ingredients

Almond-Chocolate Crescents Recipe

Ingredients:

1/4 cup almond paste

3/4 cup semisweet chocolate chips

1 tablespoon shortening

1 tube (8 ounces) refrigerated crescent rolls

Directions:

Divide almond paste into eight portions; shape each into small logs. Set aside. In a microwave, melt chocolate chips and shortening; stir until smooth.

Unroll crescent dough; separate into triangles. Spread each with 1 tablespoon chocolate mixture; set aside remaining mixture for drizzling. Place one portion almond paste at wide end of each triangle. Roll up and place point side down 2 in. apart on an ungreased baking sheet; curve ends to form a crescent.

Bake at 375° for 11-13 minutes or until golden brown. Remove to wire rack to cool completely. Drizzle with reserved chocolate mixture. Yield: 8 rolls.

Bacon-Onion Pinwheels

Ingredients:

10 slices cooked Bacon, crumbled
1 small onion, finely chopped
1/4 cup butter or margarine, softened
2 Tbsp. chopped fresh parsley
2 cans (8 oz. each) refrigerated crescent dinner rolls

Directions:

Heat oven to 375°F.

Mix all ingredients except crescent dough.

Unroll dough. Separate dough from each can into 4 rectangles; firmly press perforations together to seal. Spread dough with bacon mixture; roll up, starting at one short end of each rectangle. Cut each roll crosswise into 4 slices; place, cut sides up, 4 inches apart on baking sheets. Flatten slightly.

Bake 15 min. or until golden brown.

Little Reubens

Ingredients:

1 pkg. (16 oz.) Angus Beef Franks
2 cans (8 oz. each) refrigerated crescent dinner rolls
1 cup drained and patted dry Sauerkraut
1 cup Thousand Island Dressing
2 Tbsp Horseradish

Directions:

Heat oven to 375ºF.

Cut each frank into 6 pieces. Unroll dough into 16 triangles; cut each triangle lengthwise into thirds.

Place 1 tsp. sauerkraut and 1 frank on wide end of each triangle; roll up. Place, point-sides down, on baking sheet.

Bake 12 to 14 min. or until golden brown.

Mix dressing and horseradish; serve with franks.

Cheesy Piggies in a Blanket with Come-Back Sauce

Ingredients:

1 pkg. (8 oz.) refrigerated crescent dinner rolls
1/4 cup A.1. Original Sauce
2 KRAFT Singles, quartered
1 pkg. (16 oz.) Beef Franks
1 egg, beaten
1 tsp. poppy seed
1/4 cup Barbecue Sauce
1/4 cup Mayonnaise
4 tsp. Dijon Mustard
1-1/2 tsp. Yellow Mustard

Directions:

Heat oven to 350ºF.

Separate crescent dough into 8 triangles. Brush with steak sauce; top with Singles pieces. Place 1 frank on wide end of each dough triangle; roll up.

Place, seam-sides down, on baking sheet. Brush with egg; sprinkle with poppy seed.

Bake 10 to 12 min. or until golden brown,

Meanwhile, mix all remaining ingredients until blended.

Serve franks with sauce.

Creamy Mushroom Tartlets

Ingredients:

1 Tbsp. butter or margarine
1 pkg. (8 oz.) fresh mushrooms, finely chopped
1/2 cup Chive & Onion Cream Cheese Spread
1/4 cup Grated Parmesan Cheese
1 can (8 oz.) refrigerated crescent dinner rolls
2 tsp. finely chopped fresh parsley

Directions:

Heat oven to 350°F.

Melt butter in large nonstick skillet on medium heat. Add mushrooms; cook 5 min. or until tender, stirring frequently. Add cream cheese spread and Parmesan; cook and stir 1 min. or until cream cheese is melted. Remove from heat; set aside.

Unroll dough into 2 long rectangles; firmly press perforations and seams together to seal. Cut each rectangle into 12 squares. Place 1 square in each of 24 mini muffin cups with corners of squares extending over rims of cups. Firmly press dough onto bottom and up side of each cup. Spoon about 1-1/2 tsp. mushroom mixture into each cup.

Bake 10 to 12 min. or until golden brown. Sprinkle with parsley. Cool in pan 5 min. before serving.

Repin Crab Rangoon Crescent Cups

Ingredients:

1 package Pillsbury Crescent rolls (regular size)
4 oz cream cheese , softened
1/4 cup mayonnaise
1 1/2 teaspoons lemon juice
1/2 teaspoon Worcestershire sauce
1 green onion , finely sliced
1 can (6oz) crab meat, drained
1 clove garlic
1/2 cup & 1/3 cup mozzarella cheese (divided)

Directions:

Preheat oven to 375 degrees.

In a small bowl combine cream cheese, mayonnaise, lemon juice, Worcestershire sauce, green onion, garlic and 1/2 cup mozzarella cheese. Gently fold in crab meat and set aside.

Open crescent rolls, pinch seams together and cut into 18 even squares.

Place crescent squares in a mini muffin pan and gently press into the cups. Divide filling between wells. Top with remaining 1/3 cup cheese.

Bake 12 minutes. Allow to cool 5 minutes before removing from pan.

3-Ingredients Crescent Sausage Bites

Ingredients:

1 lb. hot sausage (pork or turkey)
1 (8 oz.) package cream cheese
2 packages crescent rolls
Dash salt & ground black pepper

Directions:

In a saute pan, brown sausage; drain. Add a dash of salt and pepper. Blend in cream cheese until the cream cheese is melted.

Unroll one package of crescent rolls and place on a baking sheet. With your fingers, gently press the seams together to seal them. Spread the sausage mixture evenly over the crescent roll dough, leaving about a 1/2-inch border along the edges.

Unroll the remaining package of crescent rolls and place on top of the sausage mixture. Press the edges together to seal. Gently press the seams together.

Bake at 375 degrees for about 20 minutes, or until crescent roll dough is golden brown.

Cut into small squares and serve

Ham and Cheese Roll-ups

Ingredients:

1 can (8 oz) Pillsbury™ refrigerated crescent dinner rolls

8 thin slices cooked ham (8 oz)

4 thin slices Cheddar cheese (4 oz), each cut into 4 strips

Directions:

Heat oven to 350°F. Separate dough into 8 triangles. Place 1 piece of ham on each triangle; place 2 strips of cheese down center of ham. Fold in edges of ham to match shape of dough triangle.

Roll up each crescent, ending at tip of triangle. Place with tips down on ungreased cookie sheet.

Bake 15 to 19 minutes or until golden brown. Immediately remove from cookie sheet. Serve warm.

Creamy Spinach Roll Ups

Ingredients:

8 oz. Cream Cheese

8 oz. Monterey Jack Cheese Shredded

1/4 tsp. Garlic Powder

1/4 Yellow Onion Diced Small

1 10 oz. Package of Frozen Spinach, Thawed and Drained Really Well

1 Box of Puff Pastry Sheets (2 Sheets)

1 Egg

1 Tbsp. Water

Directions:

Combine the Egg and Water and Beat untll well mixed.

Combine Softened Cream Cheese, Monterey Jack Cheese, Garlic Powder and Onion in a bowl and mix well.

Add Spinach into the Cream Cheese Mixture and stir.

Unroll Puff Pastry Sheets and Brush both sides with Egg and Water Mixture.

Spread Cream Cheese and Spinach Mixture over one side of the Puff Pastry.

Roll Up thc Puff Pastry and Slice.

Place rolls on a Baking Sheet and bake at 400 Degrees for 20 Minutes or until the Puff Pastry turns a golden color.

Fiesta Pinwheels

Ingredients:

1/4 cup Mexican shredded chicken

1/4 cup Green onions

Salsa

1 can Pillsbury crescent dinner rolls, refrigerated

4 tbsp Mexican four cheese blend shredded cheese

4 tbsp Sour cream

Directions:

Preheat oven to 350°F.

If using crescent rolls: Unroll dough; separate into 2 long rectangles. Press each into 12x4-inch rectangle, firmly pressing perforations to seal. If using dough sheet: Unroll dough; cut lengthwise into 2 long rectangles. Press each into 12x4-inch rectangle.

Spread 2 tablespoons of sour cream over each rectangle. Sprinkle each with half of the shredded chicken

Bake 12 to 17 minutes or until edges are deep golden brown. Immediately remove from cookie sheet. Serve warm and with salsa for dipping, if desired., cheese, and green onions.

Starting with one short side, roll up each rectangle and press the edge to seal. Using a serrated knife, cut each roll into 8 slices and place cut side down on an ungreased cookie sheet.

Bake 12 to 17 minutes or until edges are deep golden brown. Immediately remove from cookie sheet. Serve warm and with salsa for dipping, if desired.

Bacon Appetizer Crescents

Ingredients:

8 ounces Philadelphia Cream Cheese (softened)

8 slices Oscar Mayer Bacon (cooked, crumbled)

1/3 cup Kraft Grated Parmesan Cheese

1/4 cup finely chopped onion

2 tablespoons fresh parsley (chopped)

1 tablespoon milk

2 cans refrigerated crescent rolls (8 oz. each)

Directions

Heat oven to 375°F.

Mix all ingredients except crescent dough.

Separate each can of dough into 8 triangles; cut each triangle lengthwise in half. Spread each dough triangle with 1 generous tsp. cream cheese mixture; roll up, starting at short side of triangle. Place, point-sides down, on baking sheet.

Bake 12 to 15 min. or until golden brown. Serve warm.

Heat oven to 375°F.

Mix all ingredients except crescent dough.

Separate each can of dough into 8 triangles; cut each triangle lengthwise in half. Spread each dough triangle with 1 generous tsp. cream cheese mixture; roll up, starting at short side of triangle. Place, point-sides down, on baking sheet.

Bake 12 to 15 min. or until golden brown. Serve warm.

Cranberry-Cream Cheese Crescent Bites

Ingredients:

4 oz cream cheese, softened

3 tablespoons chopped dried cranberries

1 tablespoon chopped fresh chives

1 teaspoon finely diced seeded jalapeño chile

1 can (8 oz) Pillsbury™ refrigerated crescent dough sheet or 1 can (8 oz) Pillsbury™ refrigerated crescent dinner rolls

Directions:

Heat oven to 375°F. Line two cookie sheets with cooking parchment paper.

In medium bowl, mix cream cheese, cranberries, chives and jalapeño chile.

Unroll dough on work surface. Press into 12x8-inch rectangle. (If using crescent roll dough, firmly press perforations to seal.) With pizza cutter or sharp knife, cut into 6 rows by 4 rows to make 24 squares.

Place 1 teaspoon cream cheese mixture onto center of each square. Bring 4 corners together to overlap slightly in center at top of each bundle. Twist and pinch to seal, leaving small gaps between seams. Place on cookie sheets.

Bake 11 to 13 minutes or until golden brown. Serve warm.

Pepperoni and Cheese Bombs

Ingredients:

Crescent Roll Dough

2 sticks White String Cheese 2 sticks cut into 4 even pieces

Homestyle RAGÚ® Pasta Sauce (Thick and Hearty Traditional)

32 piece of pepperoni

Italian Herbs

Muffin tin

Directions:

Heat oven to 350 degrees Fahrenheit

Spray a muffin tin with non stick

Open your crescent dough and lay each triangle over an open muffin tin space

Add one teaspoon of Homestyle RAGÚ® Pasta Sauce Thick and Hearty Traditional to each triangle

Add two pieces of pepperoni, then one piece of cheese, followed by 2 more pieces to cover it

Wrap each triangle over and fold into a ball

Sprinkle with herbs

Bake for 8-10 minutes or until golden brown

Serve with an additional side of warm pasta sauce

Chili Cheddar Pinwheels

Ingredients:

1 package (8 ounces) cream cheese, softened

1 cup (4 ounces) shredded cheddar cheese

1 can (4 ounces) chopped green chilies, drained

2 tablespoons picante sauce

1/2 teaspoon chili powder

1/4 teaspoon garlic salt

1/4 teaspoon onion powder

2 tubes (8 ounces each) refrigerated crescent rolls

Additional chili powder, optional

Directions:

In a mixing bowl, beat cream cheese. Add the cheddar cheese, chilies, picante sauce, chili powder, garlic salt and onion powder. Separate each tube of crescent roll dough into four rectangles; press perforations to seal. Spread about 1/4 cup cheese mixture over each rectangle. Roll up jelly-roll style, starting with a short side. Wrap in plastic wrap and chill for at least 1 hour.

Cut each roll into eight slices; place on ungreased baking sheets. Sprinkle with additional chili powder if desired.

Bake at 350° for 10-12 minutes or until golden brown

Made in the USA
Columbia, SC
12 September 2023